TABLE OF CONTENTS

INTRODUCTION

Despite the best efforts of both the defense industry and the myriad of subject matter experts who have written books on the subject in the past decade, there has been no magic operational approach or piece of equipment unearthed that is guaranteed to defeat an insurgency. As with other forms of conflict, there remain too many variables beyond the grasp of human control, too many instances of luck, and too much uncertainty to predetermine the outcome of any given conflict. In fact, victory against an insurgency can be even more difficult to predict because it relies so heavily on the will of a population directly engaged in the conflict, rather than a more conventional conflict between two opposing armies where mathematical models and logic are more easily applied. For all the discourse and debates about population centric approaches instead of enemy centric approaches and counterinsurgency versus counterterrorism, the core issue remains how to make men stop fighting. This paper does not address how to make the individual insurgent put down his arms and walk away; rather its focus is on attacking the insurgency at the operational level.

The past decade of conflict has continued a debate that has gone through numerous peaks and valleys for the past half century: how does a military force defeat an opponent displaying asymmetric organization and capabilities? Following rapid victories during the initial phases of both Afghanistan and Iraq, the United States confronted insurgencies in both countries that frustrated their efforts to transition authority. Al-Qaeda (AQ) continues to remain relevant in the Arab world and has expanded its operations to Northern Africa despite over a decade of war with the United States and the death of many of their senior leaders. Israel has conducted numerous operations against Hamas and Hezbollah over the past decade, including their failed operations in southern Lebanon in 2006. Even in the Pacific, a region that the United States has stated that it will rebalance its efforts towards, multiple nations continue to combat a myriad of transnational

1

terrorist and internal insurgent organizations. These operational challenges and the often-ambiguous nature of the "peace" that follows have renewed a policy debate of how best to approach operations against rogue state and non-state actors.

Recent policy statements indicate that US forces will no longer be manned to a level that will facilitate long-term stability operations, further strengthening the narrative that fighting insurgents is not the job of the United States.[1] However, it is unrealistic to assume that the United States will never become involved in another conflict involving insurgents given the level of instability in regions of vital national interest such as Asia, Africa, and the Middle East. These areas present a number of potential flash points that the United States may be called to either support a partner nation or assume a stabilizing role in the aftermath of a revolution. In either of those instances, the ability to properly frame the operational environment and design an operational approach that rapidly reestablishes stability will be critical to strategic success.

Current counterinsurgency doctrine focuses the attention of commanders away from affecting change on the enemy and on affecting the environmental conditions that surround the enemy and the population. This was function of attempting to correct the uneven approaches in the early phases of Operation Iraqi Freedom while instilling the core idea that a more holistic approach to the problem was needed. Unfortunately, this attempt at expanding understanding led in many ways to a dogmatic approach to countering insurgency, with commanders looking for a cut and paste solution to operational problems rather than countering the specific enemy in front of them. The theoretical concept that guides this idea dictates that through creating change in the environment, the counterinsurgent will deny the insurgency the ability to regenerate and survive.

Sadly, this monograph yet again fails to offer a panacea for the ills that befall potential counterinsurgents. This monograph does not propose an end all, be all solution for the defeat and

---

[1] US, Department Of Defense, *Sustaining U.S. Global Leadership: Priorities for the 21ˢᵗ Century Defense* (Washington DC: January 2012), 6.

destruction of an insurgent organization. The focus of this work is to ascertain whether the concept of operational shock, what has served as the intellectual underpinning of the US Army's doctrine over the past thirty years, can be used to guide an operational approach in a counterinsurgency campaign. This work attempts to provide operational level planners a mental model to use in the description of both an insurgency and the effects that the counterinsurgent forces are attempting to create.

Research Questions and Scope

Throughout this monograph, the term "operational shock" will be defined as placing the rival in a position where they are both cognitively and physically unable to act due to the effect of the friendly force's operations. The primary research question for this study is whether a counterinsurgent force can impose operational shock on an opponent displaying asymmetric organization and tactics. The secondary research question is to identify the characteristics of a counterinsurgency campaign that is capable of imposing shock. The monograph uses insurgency as the vehicle to illustrate the point, as many terrorist organizations such as al-Qaeda and so-called "hybrid" threats such as Hezbollah exhibit similar traits of a classical insurgency. The individual characteristics of the concept must be modified to the specific threat, but the intellectual scaffolding remains the same.

Methodology

The study will use systems theory and complexity theory to define the operational environment and explain the interactions between opponents in several historical campaigns against insurgents. Additionally, it examines classical and emerging theories of insurgency and the methods that various counterinsurgents have used to disrupt or defeat their opponent. Finally, this monograph will identify the most important interactions that a successful counterinsurgency campaign must influence in order to place an insurgency in a condition of operational shock.

The study begins with a literature review, which will be divided into five sections. The first section of the literature review examines the evolution of the theory of operational shock, general systems theory, complexity theory, and complex adaptive systems. This section introduces G.S Isserson, Shimon Naveh, and John Boyd's theories during this section in order to display the evolution of the concept of operational shock; from a systematic approach to conducting maneuver warfare to a systemic approach to causing the collapse of an enemy system. The second section of the literature review focuses on the theories surrounding insurgency and the contemporary view of counterinsurgent warfare. The purpose of this review is to describe how the United States views the problem of insurgent warfare and analyze how it developed its primary counterinsurgency doctrine, US Army Field Manual 3-24: *Counterinsurgency*, published in 2006. Theories from prominent counterinsurgency scholars will be examined as well as the traditional operational approaches of enemy centric and population centric counterinsurgency. In addition to these broad approaches, the study will include alternative theories of control and operational approaches, as these principles will also be applied during the case study portion of the study.

The final section of the literature review explains the theory of operational shock as applied to an insurgency. This section synthesizes elements from Isserson, Naveh, and Boyd with theories of counterinsurgency to propose an alternative perspective for attacking insurgent networks. This section highlights the characteristics of an insurgent system in a state of shock and discusses methods the counterinsurgent can use to achieve this effect. This theory does not suppose to prescribe a method for final victory in a counterinsurgency campaign. Rather, it is focused on methods to make the insurgency temporarily unable to significantly affect the work towards this long-term development. Essentially, it is to buy time for the political processes essential for lasting victory to take affect.

Following the literature review are two case studies that use Alexander George's

4

comparative case study method to examine historical case studies. Each case study will examine a historical counterinsurgency campaign in the same fashion. First, the case study will briefly describe the strategic context of the campaign and then describe the nature of the insurgency. Next, the counterinsurgent's operational approach is examined. Finally, each case study examines the traits of operational shock expressed by the insurgency. The selected case studies will reflect the anticipated operational environment that American forces will likely encounter when dealing with insurgency; namely hegemonic powers conducting a campaign in an expeditionary manner to assist a partnered government force against an insurgent organization.

The final section of the monograph serves as a conclusion to the study and addresses potential implications of the findings. The conclusion will analyze the operational approaches from both of the campaigns from the previous chapters, combine those with the theories from the literature review, and highlight characteristics that facilitated the application of shock. Finally, this section will identify areas of further inquiry for operational planners and researchers.

LITERATURE REVIEW

Operational Shock

The concept of operational shock is rooted in maneuver warfare and was originally
applied in a conventional context; however, it is the idea itself that is important to this study.
Operational shock is achieved when an opponent is both cognitively and physically unable to act
due to the effect of an opposing force's operations. The concept of operational shock originated
from Russian theorists in the post World War I era and has informed much of the doctrine of both
the United States and the Israeli Defense Forces in the modern era.[2] Much like the
counterinsurgent, Russian operational planers faced opponents they may not be able to destroy
due to the size of the opponent and dispersion that modern armies displayed. Theorists such as
G.S. Isserson sought methods to avoid the attritional warfare of the First World War and achieve
victory through dominant maneuver and overwhelming their opponent.[3]

Isserson advocated the systematic elimination of a rival's options through the
overwhelming actions Soviet forces across the width and depth of the battlefield. Isserson's
theory sought to penetrate the front line defenses of his opponent, and then exploit this
penetration point with mechanized forces. These mechanized forces were designed for speed and
maneuver and would seize key logistics bases, command nodes, and rail networks, denying the
enemy the ability to operationally maneuver his forces.[4] This rapid maneuver, coupled with
attacks along multiple layers of the enemy's defense would confuse and render him unable to
continue to command at the operational level. The core concepts of "deep operations" informed

---

[2] Dima Adamsky, *The Culture of Military Innovation: the Impact of Cultural Factors On the Revolution in Military Affairs in Russia, the US, and Israel* (Stanford, Calif.: Stanford Security Studies, 2010), 101.

[3] Shimon Naveh, *In Pursuit of Military Excellence: The Evolution of Operational Theory* (Portland: Frank Cass, 1997), 16.

[4] G.S. Isserson, *"The Evolution of Operational Art,"* Translated by Bruce W. Menning (Fort Leavenworth, KS: SAMS Theoretical Special Edition, 2005).

not only Soviet doctrine in World War II, but also the famed AirLand battle doctrine the United States built in the 1980s to counter the Soviet threat in Eastern Europe. This doctrine was successfully exported beyond its primary intent and used with great success in Operation Desert Storm.

In the post-Vietnam era of transformation within the US Army, similar conceptions of shock began to permeate throughout the force. Faced with the challenge of defending against a massive Soviet army in the plains of Europe, American commanders sought a way to inflict massive amounts of damage against the structure of their opponent and affect them at the operational level.[5] John Boyd, an American Air Force officer, discussed this effort in detail through his numerous writings and presentations. Though Boyd never wrote a definitive work, he was a prolific speaker and theorist, becoming famous for his Observe-Orient-Decide-Act (OODA) loop. However, Boyd's theories expanded well beyond just this graphical depiction and centered on creating a systemic collapse of an opponent by physically, morally, and mentally isolating them from their allies, internal and external support.[6] Using scientific laws such as the second law of thermodynamics to illustrate his theories, Boyd discussed creating friction within the enemy's system and delaying the enemy's decision-making cycle. He believed that success in conflict revolved around time, and that by increasing the friendly force's time to understand the situation and by decreasing your opponent's time to understand, you create greater friction within the enemy's system. This friction will increase the pressure and isolation on the rival system, eventually causing the rival to be unable to sustain operations and succumb to their opponent's will.

---

[5] Adamsky, 61.

[6] Frans Osinga, *Science, Strategy and War: The Strategic Theory of John Boyd* (London: Routledge, 2006), 213. Boyd's description of winning consists of inflicting physical, moral, and mental isolation of your opponent, while increasing your own interactions within and outside of your own system.

The next evolution in the theory of operational shock originated from Israeli brigadier general Shimon Naveh. He attempted to expand Isserson's theories and the American interpretation of operational art, while integrating the science of systems theory into his interpretation of operational shock. Naveh defined the military organization itself as the system; the command structures, the tension between orders and actions, the ability to move and communicate, the ability to project and absorb damage, and its ability to achieve its purpose. Naveh stated that the "significance of attrition lies solely in its auxiliary service to the manoeuvre."[7] Naveh also argued that with the size and lethality of modern armies, achieving total destruction of an enemy force was now impossible, therefore the method to achieving victory on the modern battlefield was through the disaggregation of the enemy at the systemic level.

Naveh's theory of operational shock states that the aggressor must overwhelm his opponent's ability to deal with the number, tempo, and severity of the strikes applied against his operational structure. His concept includes both physical and cognitive assaults on the enemy's system; attacks on the opponent's forces and positions themselves and also attacks on the opponent's understanding and rationale for continuing the conflict. The goal of the physical attacks is to create "division or fragmentation" of the enemy's structures, bringing about the collapse of his ability to continue to fight.[8] He rejects the assertion he associates with Clausewitzian logic that to defeat an opponent, you must destroy his forces.[9] Instead, he posits that the key to defeating one's opponent and the focus of the operational artist must be the

---

[7] Naveh, 23.

[8] Naveh, 17.

[9] This explanation of Clausewitz's logic is Naveh's, from the introduction of *In Pursuit of Military Excellence.* This is odd, as much of what Naveh is discussing is nested with Clausewitz's assertion that the focus of your operation is your opponent's forces, his will, or his territory (space). Naveh describes a similar approach, but his focus is on the will and the space as opposed to destroying the forces themselves.

disruption the opponent's rationale to continue to fight. The decisive maneuver serves to physically separate the enemy's various echelons of command and increase the "cognitive tension" between the actors in the system. This cognitive tension represents the difference between the intent of the commander at the strategic or operational level, and the ability for tactical movement by his subordinate commanders. Naveh posits that by increasing the amount of tension on the system through creating a spatial and intellectual disadvantage, the enemy system will eventually collapse.

Systems Theory

To develop a greater understanding of Boyd and Naveh's theories, a basic explanation of General Systems Theory is required. A system is simply a description of the relationship of things that interact.[10] The two basic types of systems are closed and open systems. Closed systems do not exchange energy with their environment, serve a limited number of purposes, and have a predetermined output.[11] It has been argued that there is no such thing as a completely closed system, as everything interacts with its environment in some way. An open system is one that exchanges energy with its surrounding environment through a series of positive and negative feedback mechanisms. As the environmental conditions around and inside a system change, this is called positive feedback. The actions by the system to preserve it and adapt to those changing conditions is known as negative feedback. The key to survival for a system is its ability to rapidly adapt and provide negative feedback against the positive feedback. A system that can do this effectively is referred to as a robust system, while those that cannot are generally referred to as weak systems. Both Boyd and Naveh's theories seek to overwhelm the opponent's negative

---

[10] Alexander Laszlo et al, *Systems Theories: Their Origins, Foundations, and Development* (Amsterdam: Elsevier Science, 1998), 47-74.

[11] Ibid., 53.

feedback loops through the continuous application of positive energies at the critical nodes. Social systems, such as insurgent organizations, military formations, and populations, are inherently open systems and are the focus of this study.

Complicating our ability to control and predict what an open system will do are the theories of chaos and complexity. Chaos theory, which is illustrated by the famous "butterfly effect" of weather patterns, attempts to describe why there are often unintended consequences to seemingly unrelated actions. Chaotic systems display what is called "sensitivity to initial conditions," meaning that the initial state of the system will have dramatic impacts on the system's output.[12] These systems will often display behavior that can be referred to as non-linear, or seemingly not conforming to a rational sequence. However, simply because the outcomes do not appear to be logical to an outside observer does not mean that they are not informed by the rationale that bounds the system and dictates the interaction of the variables. All systems have an aim, or a purpose, and their actions are guided towards achieving that purpose.[13]

Because a system is chaotic does not necessarily mean that it is complex, and vice versa; however, there are many similarities between the two.[14] Complexity science describes the interrelation of multiple variables, all of which have an effect on the overall system[15]. The number of variables does not make a system complex; rather it is the interactions between those variables that are the driving factor of the complexity. In short, a complex system is greater than

---

[12] Antoine Bousquet, *The Scientific Way of Warfare: Order and Chaos on the Battlefields of Modernity* (New York, NY: Columbia Univeristy Press, 2009), 171.

[13] Jamshid Gharajedaghi, *Systems Thinking: Managing Chaos and Complexity; Second Edition* (Elsevier: Butterworth-Heinemann, 2006), 33.

[14] Neil Johnson, *Simply Complexity: A Clear Guide to Complexity Theory* (Oxford, England: One World Publications, 2009), 39.

[15] Dietrich Dorner, *The Logic of Failure: Recognizing and Avoiding Error in Complex Situations* (New York, NY: Metropolitan Books, 1996), 38.

the sum of its parts and the interactions within that system dictate its behavior.

A complex system operates in several different states: equilibrium, bifurcation, and chaos.[16] The system is at a state of equilibrium during normal functions with little to no outside stimulus. However, as more stimulation is applied to the system, the system will reach what is know as the bifurcation point; the point when the system creates an adaptation to deal with the changing conditions. As the system continues to receive positive inputs, it continues to reach bifurcation points and adapt. Finally, when the stimulus becomes too much for the system's feedback mechanisms to control, the system moves into a state of chaos and reorganization. An "attractor," or condition within the environment that pulls the system towards a new structure and purpose drives this reorganization.[17] As the system reorganizes around this new attractor, it moves back to a state of equilibrium and the process begins again.

Other key attributes of a complex system are emergence, adaptability, and self-organization.[18] Emergence is the result of the interaction of the variables within a system, and is only exhibited when the variables interact with one another. The emergent phenomena that arises from a system is unpredictable and seemingly random because none of the variables would exhibit this behavior when isolated from the system; however, when the parts of the system interact, or an external stimulus is applied, new reactions emerge.[19] Within a complex system, causality cannot be isolated to one variable, as it is not the individual variable's adaptation that is important but rather how that variable influences the emergent traits of the system. As the system continues to come in contact with its surrounding environment, it will attempt to adapt in an

---

[16] Bousquet, 177.

[17] Gharajedaghi, 52.

[18] Johnson, 14-16.

[19] Ibid., 4.

effort to make its interaction more efficient. Self-organization, or autopoiesis, refers to the variables within a system providing positive and negative feedback to each other and generating energies for themselves.

While Boyd and Naveh's theories of shock and systemic collapse were originally focused on confronting conventional military threats, their logic can be carried forward and applied to irregular opponents. In his 2010 work, *Counterinsurgency,* theorist David Kilcullen advocates a system-based approach to analyzing and attacking an insurgency.[20] Kilcullen refers to an insurgency as a complex adaptive system and uses this as the metaphor to guide his counterinsurgency approach. Kilcullen does not believe that an insurgent system is as susceptible to shock as a purely conventional opponent, however he focuses on the maneuver aspects of operational shock rather than addressing it at a conceptual level.[21] The next section of the literature review will focus on the form and function of insurgencies and the implications of applying systems logic to counterinsurgency operations.

Insurgency

While insurgency has long been a part of warfare, it was not until the late 19th and early 20th centuries that theorists began to explore more effective means of dealing with this method of making war. Following World War II, there have been insurgencies in Iraq, Afghanistan, the Philippines, Oman, Algeria, Northern Ireland, Vietnam, and Columbia, with numerous others not listed. This section of the literature review focuses on defining and describing insurgency through current doctrine and two modern insurgency theorists, examining the environmental conditions that allow for a successful insurgency, and it will describe the operational approaches

---

[20] David Kilcullen, *Counterinsurgency* (Oxford: Oxford University Press, 2010), 194.

[21] Ibid, 205.

and methods that insurgencies employ against both security forces and the population. Finally, this section of the study will briefly examine the concept of the hybrid threat as it provides a more current context that informs the thinking of US Army senior leadership.

The first thing to be addressed must be the insurgency itself. There are many varied of definitions of insurgency, but for the purposes of this study it will be confined to the doctrinal definition found in US Army Field Manual (FM) 3-24: *Counterinsurgency*. FM 3-24 defines an insurgency as an "organized, protracted politico-military struggle designed to weaken the control and legitimacy of an established government, occupying power, or other political authority while increasing insurgent control."[22] This broad definition encompasses the many types of insurgencies, each with unique aims and methods to achieve those aims. The models outlined in FM 3-24 are the Maoist, focoist, urban guerilla, and the recent form of insurgency involving religious extremists.[23] Bard O'Neill goes beyond these models and describes nine different models of insurgency: anarchist, egalitarian, traditionalist, pluralist, apocalyptic-utopian, secessionist, reformist, preservationist, and commercialist.[24] These models are not all-inclusive, however they do provide an initial framework from which to build.

As referenced in the previous section, Kilcullen described an insurgency as a social system that is complex and adaptive to the conditions around it.[25] The system is composed of

---

[22] US Army Field Manual 3-24, *Counterinsurgency* (Washington, DC: Headquarters, Department of the Army, December 2006), Pg. 1-1.

[23] Ibid, 1-4. The Maoist model of "People's War" is the most extensively discussed in both FM 3-24 and FM 3-24.2: *Tactics in Counterinsurgency*. Specifically, Mao's three phases: latent/incipient, guerilla war, and war of movement are discussed in depth.

[24] Bard E. O'Neill, *Insurgency & Terrorism: from Revolution to Apocalypse*, 2nd ed. (Washington, D.C.: Potomac Books Inc., 2005), 19.

[25] Kilcullen, *Counterinsurgency,* 194.

nodes, links, boundaries, subsystems, boundary interactions, inputs, and outputs.[26] Nodes are the actual physical structures around which the system is built and can be as narrowly defined as an individual leader or as broadly defined as is useful for analysis such as a cell or organizational function. The links highlight the interactions within the insurgency and also the interactions beyond its internal boundaries and into its surrounding environment. Subsystems refer to the "systems within systems," such as leadership networks, financial systems, and supply networks. The inputs and outputs are the exchanges of energies between the insurgency and its environment. Both the insurgent system and that of the counterinsurgent are struggling the control of these inputs and outputs through the influence of the linkages. The insurgents, the counterinsurgents, the host nation, and to a lesser degree the international community, all serve as subsystems within the larger system, which defines the operational environment.

David Galula states that for an insurgent system to thrive, four conditions must be present within the operational environment: a cause that resonated with the population, a weak counterinsurgent force, favorable geographic conditions, and external support.[27] Galula is essentially describing the environmental frame that the insurgency and the governmental forces both operate within and try to manipulate through their operations.[28] The strength or weakness of these conditions make up the "fitness" of the insurgent system, a concept that will be addressed again later in the section.

For the insurgent system, the cause serves as this aim and is the organizing feature around which it is built. Galula states that the cause is the political or social condition that is at the core

---

[26] Ibid., 196-197.

[27] David Galula, *Counterinsurgency Warfare: Theory and Practice* (Saint Petersburg, FL: Glenwood Press, 1964), 17-42.

[28] The term "environmental frame" is used here to reflect current US Army doctrine, which discusses the environmental frame as one visualization tool as part of the Army Design Methodology. For a detailed discussion of the ADM, see Chapter 2 of Army Doctrinal Reference Publication 5-0.

of the insurgent problem; in essence it is the disease and the insurgency is the symptom of that disease. The identification of the root cause and an understanding of the type of insurgent organization that one is confronted with will provide a clearer appreciation of the goals and methods the insurgency will use to achieve them. Bard O'Neill states that the "whatever the difficulty, ascertaining the goals of insurgent organizations is a crucial first step in any analysis."[29] However, as O'Neill and Galula point out, the aims of the insurgency will continually morph and their actions or those of the counterinsurgent change as the conditions around them also change.[30] As referenced during the discussion of systems theory, the cause serves as the "attractor" that the insurgent system moves towards during periods of adaptation. Galula states that the cause is very important as the insurgency is beginning, but as it gains strength the original cause becomes less important over time.[31] It is unlikely that the insurgent system will change its aim or purpose entirely, but rather adapt their methods it will take to achieve those aims.

The second environmental condition that influences the insurgency is the strength of the counterinsurgent. One of the core principles of counterinsurgency theory is to control the population in an effort to separate them from the insurgents. As Galula states, if the insurgency has leadership and a cause to rally around, it is irrelevant if the government they wish to overthrow has the means to put the insurgency down.[32] The United States traditionally places security sector development as a top priority during counterinsurgency campaigns, as witnessed in Vietnam, Iraq, and Afghanistan. However, the physical strength of the government, manifested

---

[29] O'Neill, 31.

[30] Ibid, 29.

[31] Galula, 25.

[32] Ibid., 15.

15

in the security forces, does not translate into its ability to govern and provide for the population it wishes to control. A counterinsurgent force that is not native to the country, as the United States has been in all its counterinsurgency efforts since the American Civil War, also suffers from a multitude of inherent weaknesses.[33] While the United States owned a distinct advantage in military capability in both Iraq and Afghanistan, the insurgencies in both cases exploited disadvantages such as the lack of cultural understanding, religious differences, American overuse of force, and sectarian differences within the native populations, to create positions of weakness within the American effort.

Despite advances in technologies such as unmanned aerial vehicles and satellite imagery, terrain and geography still remain a consideration for the counterinsurgent. Galula posits that the more difficult the terrain and the more natural barriers exist, the more this favors the insurgent.[34] However, Galula is not only concerned with the terrain; the size of the country, location, population number and density, and economic conditions all play a role in the geographic considerations. The tension between political ideology and religious ideology, the overlapping of major ethnic and religious groups, and the location and distribution of natural resources within the country are also factors in this calculus. However, the effects of globalization in recent years have changed this dynamic to a degree. Kilcullen describes a modern insurgency operating in a "virtual state," essentially operating across boundaries with little regard to their meaning or restrictions.[35] Insurgencies now have an ability to interact with supporters and leadership much

---

[33] This condition is referred to as operating as a "third party counterinsurgent." The concept is that any external actor, especially one with a different culture/language/religion, which attempts to intervene on behalf of one of the belligerents in an insurgency, is operating as a third party in the conflict. Just as the counterinsurgents are attempting to isolate the insurgent organization from their external support, a major goal of the insurgent is to force a disaggregation of the host nation government and the external actor.

[34] Ibid., 36.

[35] Kilcullen, *Counterinsurgency,* 200.

easier and from greater distances. Despite this, the insurgency must still understand the social and ethical "boundaries" of the social system it is trying to influence. The challenge for the operational planner now becomes defining the scope at which to assess the geographic conditions in a manner that makes them useful.

The final condition this study will focus on is the external support for the insurgency. The term external does not only refer to support from outside the country, but all support from outside of the insurgent system. The passive or active support of the population, financial support, and moral support are all components of external support.[36] The boundary interactions, as described by Kilcullen and referenced earlier in this study, are the manifestation of this external support. While this support base can serve as a source of strength for the insurgency, it also is one of their critical vulnerabilities as the external support of the insurgency is often the primary target amongst counterinsurgents. As a counterinsurgent attempts to cause change within an insurgency, it is the nature of the enemy's interactions and links with this external support that the counterinsurgent must address. If the insurgent system is isolated from its support systems either physically or cognitively, the insurgent system loses the ability to regenerate and adapt. The counterinsurgent can now begin to create and exploit breakdowns within the insurgent system itself.

Though it is true that the insurgencies France, England, and the United States were fighting in the 1950s and 1960s were more politically defined than the recent wave of Islamist-based insurgencies, the objectives of the insurgencies in Iraq and Afghanistan have been no less political. In Iraq, both JAM and al-Qaeda-in-Iraq (AQI) sought to expel the Americans in order to overthrow the government and establish an Islamist government. Even more so, in Afghanistan the Taliban were at one time the sitting power and are now fighting to regain that

---

[36] Galula, 20.

17

power. It is irrelevant that their political ideology is religious based vice political theory based; the end state is still the same for both insurgencies. The conditions for a successful insurgency, as Galula describes them, are all displayed in current operations. In fact, David Kilcullen describes the current conflict with terrorist organizations as a "global insurgency" and advocates a counterinsurgent approach to dealing with the problem.[37] The variance is expressed in the methods and the tactics employed by the present day insurgents, as dictated by their access to weaponry and support, and the impact of their cultural approach to fighting.

Insurgents can employ a wide variety of methods, from limited terrorist attacks to offensive operations displaying combined arms maneuver, to achieve their political or ideological ends. Additionally, all insurgent operations have three intended targets: the population, the counterinsurgent, and their supporters. In 1987, Yasser Arafat and the Palestinian Liberation Organization (PLO) helped organize a mixture of non-lethal operations, protests, small attacks, and press coverage that eventually led to significant concessions from the Israelis in 1993.[38] Abu Musab Zarqawi, the leader of al-Qaeda's affiliate in Iraq, attempted to incite a civil war between the Shia and the Sunni populations in an attempt to first drive the Americans from Iraq and then to establish Baghdad as the capital of the new Islamic caliphate.[39] Both of these are examples of very different approaches of insurgent leaders. The strongest insurgencies adjust their operational approach based on the relative strength of the conditions necessary for their success as expressed by Galula in order to remain aligned with their strategic goals and to capitalize on the changing

[37] Kilcullen, *Counterinsurgency,* 165-226. Though Kilcullen is often identified with a population centric approach through his work with GEN David Petraeus in Iraq, his strategy of disaggregation is decidedly enemy focused.

[38] Thomas X. Hammes, *The Sling and the Stone: On War in the 21st Century* (Mechanicsburg, PA: Zenith Press, 2006), 89-110.

[39] Seth G. Jones, *Hunting in the Shadows: the Pursuit of Al Qa'ida Since 9/11* (New York: W. W. Norton & Company, 2012), 150-151.

environment. The weakest insurgencies do not vary their approaches and are therefore destroyed very early on in the fighting or never achieve any meaningful gains.

Since 2006, there has been renewed interest in what has been termed the "hybrid threat." In its newest series of doctrinal manuals, the United States Army defines the hybrid threat as "the diverse and dynamic combination of regular forces, irregular forces, terrorist forces, and/or criminal elements unified to achieve mutually benefitting effects."[40] During the Second Lebanon War in 2006, Hezbollah forces operating from inside Lebanon inflicted severe damage on Israel's vaunted armored formations and prevented Israeli units from seizing key objectives by employing a mixture of conventional and unconventional methods. The Israeli forces, underprepared to fight a conventional battle, were badly embarrassed and eventually agreed to a ceasefire.[41] Though several commentators have approached this as the making of a new security threat, the reality is that the hybrid model is one that has been used repeatedly throughout history, including in World War II, the American Revolution, the Franco-Prussian War, and Vietnam.[42] In fact, the mixture of these approaches merely represents a transitional period between Phase II, guerilla warfare, and Phase III, war of movement, of Mao's three phase People's War model. So while modern technology provides the hybrid threat a variety of weaponry and capabilities, its foundational concepts are still nested within historical patterns of insurgency.

Counterinsurgent Theory

The preponderance of counterinsurgency theory focuses on causing a separation between the insurgency and the population, though the methods will vary. The vast majority of this

---

[40] U.S. Department of the Army, *Army Doctrine Reference Publication 3-0, Unified Land Operations*, 2012, 1-3.

[41] Matt M. Matthews, *We Were Caught Unprepared: The 2006 Hezbollah-Israeli War* (Leavenworth, KS, 2008).

[42] Williamson Murray and Peter R. Mansoor, *Hybrid Warfare: Fighting Complex Opponents from the Ancient World to the Present* (New York: Cambridge University Press, 2012.

literature was written in the mid 20th century, as western nations such as France and England encountered insurgencies within former colonies. Authors such as David Galula, Frank Kitson, and Robert Thompson all contributed well-known works to the body of knowledge and many of their methods and principles still live in doctrinal concepts of both the American and British Army.[43] During the past decade, there has been a renewed interest in studying insurgency and in countering those insurgencies. Social scientists such as Montgomery McFate and Sebastian Gorka, as well as soldiers turned scholars David Kilcullen and John Nagl are all amongst the writers leading this renewal. While the purpose of this monograph is not to review the principles prescribed in the various doctrines, it is important to understand two of the competing paradigms associated with the prosecution of counterinsurgency operations: population centric and enemy centric.

The most popular expression of counterinsurgent warfare in recent years has been the population centric approach. The population centric approach focuses the efforts on addressing the needs of the population and trying to connect the population to the government and drawing them away from the insurgency. As Galula identifies, the counterinsurgent must address the cause of the insurgency and then limit its resonance with the population. This cause can be economic disparity, governmental control, or religious ideology, amongst many possible reasons.[44] The population centric approach focuses on securing the population in order to separate them from the insurgents and then addressing the root causes of the conflict from within. Tools such as the Tactical Conflict Assessment Planning Framework (TCAPF) are implemented

---

[43] Galula, a French officer, wrote *Counterinsurgency in Modern Warfare: Theory and Practice.* Sir Robert Thompson, a British veteran of Burma and the campaign in Malaysia wrote *Countering Communist Insurgency.* Frank Kitson, another British officer whose service began after the Second World War and was heavily influenced by the anti colonial insurgencies of the 1950s and 1960s, wrote numerous works, primary amongst them are *Low Intensity Operations* and *Bunch of Five.*

[44] Galula, 21.

to assist commanders in understanding and addressing the root causes of internal conflict within their operational environments. [45] The phrase "the population is the center of gravity" is borne of this operational approach, as all actions by the counterinsurgent force should be focused on addressing the conditions of the population, and that by improving these conditions the counterinsurgent force can defeat the insurgency.

Population centric counterinsurgency has become synonymous with a long-term endeavor that requires massive investments of personnel and money on the part of the counterinsurgent. Its strength lies in that, if successful, it sets conditions for long-term stability for the country and governmental forces. A successfully executed population centric campaign attacks the insurgent problem from multiple angles, such as establishing services, police forces, and strengthening the host nation government. However, the weakness in this approach is that a purely population centric approach does little to address the actual insurgent forces operating in the operational environment. If the counterinsurgent does not establish security and account for the activities of the insurgency, their efforts to link the population to the government will be for naught. Also, there are times when the best interests of the government and the best interests of the population are not aligned and this can create tension within the counterinsurgent's efforts. [46]

---

[45] TCAPF is a variant of the US government's Interagency Conflict Assessment Framework (ICAF). It was tested in Iraq starting in late 2007 and widely used in Afghanistan in 2009-2010 as GEN McChrystal directed a "population centric" approach. The assessment tool is in the form of a questionnaire administered by a soldier on patrol. There are four questions asked each time: has the number of people in the village changed in the last year, what are the most important problems facing the village, who do you believe can solve your problems, what can be done to help the village? Each question is followed up with the question "why." The responses are recorded and reported to higher headquarters for analysis. The goal is to collate the data and determine what the root causes of instability in the village are and if the counterinsurgent is addressing those problems through their actions.

[46] A present day representation of this are the Sons of Iraq (SOI) and Afghan Local Police (ALP) programs introduced in Iraq and Afghanistan, respectively. Both programs were very popular with local Iraqis and Afghans as they provided a mechanism for the local leaders to provide their own security and employ members of their community. However, both programs were seen as potential threats to the federal government and highlighted the inability of the government to bring security to the population.

By contrast, enemy centric counterinsurgency focuses its efforts on the defeat of the insurgent movement by the elimination of the enemy's forces. Large clearance operations against insurgent strongholds, raids against insurgent leadership, and attempts to isolate and destroy the enemy forces are trademarks of this approach.[47] There are few modern expressions of this approach, and fewer still where the counterinsurgent has been successful. The Nazis attempted to confront the partisan movement in western Russia during World War II through a heavy-handed approach, and likely cost themselves the opportunity to turn the population in those areas against the Soviet Union, which contributed to their eventual defeat on the eastern front.[48] Forty years later those same Soviets attempted to combat an insurgency in Afghanistan with modern firepower and maneuverability, only to find frustration and eventual defeat. The strength of focusing the military efforts on disrupting and destroying the enemy's forces is that is simplifies the equation for the military commanders; search and destroy. However, history has shown that the simple destruction of insurgent forces is not effective, and often creates more insurgents in the long term.[49]

US Army doctrine recommends three approaches to a counterinsurgency operation: clear-hold-build, combined actions, and limited support.[50] Clear-hold-build, by far the most well known, provided a framework for many of the operations the US conducted in Iraq and Afghanistan. In the clear phase, counterinsurgent forces conduct operations in contested areas, targeting insurgents and establishing bases in order to defeat and disrupt insurgent organizations

---

[47] This is not to infer that these type operations are not present in a population centric campaign. Rather, these operations exist in both frameworks. The diffe

[48] Kilcullen, *Counterinsurgency,* 6.

[49] GEN Stanley McChrystal, in his discussions with subordinate commanders when he was the commander of the International Security Assistance Forces in Afghanistan referred to this as "insurgent math." The counterinsurgent force kills two insurgents but create ten more in his place because of their methods.

[50] FM 3-24, 5-18.

and deny them access to the population. The counterinsurgent forces then remain in these areas and protect the population while continuing to gather intelligence and target the insurgent structure. The final step, build, comes once security has been established to an acceptable level and service projects and programs can be established to address the root causes of instability in an area. This approach was famously advocated and employed by GEN David Petraeus and the United States Forces during the "surge" operations in 2007-2008 in Iraq. Units in both Afghanistan and Iraq have also used an additional step, shape, to describe the operations undertaken in preparation before the clearance mission. This approach is also commonly referred to as the "ink spot" approach.

Two lesser-known approaches are combined action and limited support. Combined action, as demonstrated by the Combined Action Program of the US Marine Corps in Vietnam, involves the integration of host nation security forces with US units in order to conduct security operations as well as improve the operational effectiveness of the host nation.[51] Combined action was employed in the International Security Assistance Force's Regional Command-East beginning in 2009, in an effort to improve the existing Afghan Army units. This technique can employed in conjunction with clear-hold-build, or following a successful clearance of an area. Limited support does not involve large numbers of US personnel or resources, and therefore will not be examined in great detail for this study.

Stathis Kalyvas offers an additional perspective of ways to combat and defeat insurgent organizations in his work, *The Logic of Violence In Civil War*. While Kalyvas intended for his work to focus on civil wars, many of his conclusions can be exported to counterinsurgency operations. He argues that civil war, or insurgent war, differs from interstate conflict in that the

---

[51] FM 3-24, 5-25.

violence is much more visceral and local.[52] His central thesis is that, in a civil war, the population will side with the force that can display a monopoly on violence and be the most selective in their application of violence within contested areas. To increase the ability to apply selective violence, the government (or insurgent) must increase their degree of control within an area by physically occupying the space. The main battles of insurgent warfare exist in these contested areas as both forces attempt to deny the other the intelligence necessary to target and attack their forces, while forcing the population to choose a side.[53]

Kalyvas' theory is similar to that of Boyd, as the forces are continually trying to increase their ability to move and understand, while isolating their opponent and denying them the information they need to make effective decisions.[54] Kalyvas also incorporates both aspects of population and enemy centric counterinsurgent approaches. He understands that the only way to fully defeat an insurgent force is the destruction of their armed wing, but he also addresses the requirement to address the needs of the population, with protection being the primary requirement.[55]

In summary, the majority of counterinsurgency theory is centered on control and is focused on addressing the interactions between the population and the government. Control of

---

[52] Stathis N. Kalyvas, *The Logic of Violence in Civil War* (New York: Cambridge University Press, 2006), 338.

[53] Kalyvas, 204. Kalyvas envisions five "zones" in his theory. Zones one is under the control of the "incumbents" while zone five is under the control of the insurgent. Zones two and four are contested, but dominated for the most part by the incumbents and the insurgents respectively. Zone three is the most heavily contested of the zones, and is the most difficult for both insurgent and incumbent to exercise selective violence against the other.

[54] Osinga, 214. This assertion is based on Osinga's retelling of Boyd's theory of isolation: the key to winning is to physically, mentally, and morally isolate the opponents by severing their ability to communicate both internally and externally, present them with problems that are ambiguous, and force them to act in their own interest rather than in the interests of their allies. By challenging the insurgent for control of an area, the counterinsurgent can begin to isolate the insurgent system.

[55] Kalyvas, 167.

the population, control of terrain, and control of the insurgent's actions are all components of both enemy and population centric approaches. The most successful counterinsurgency campaigns have contained a mixture of both approaches throughout the course of the effort, with conditions dictating the most appropriate course. While long-term victory is achieved by changing the nature of the interaction between the population and the government, the way in which the insurgent organization interacts with and perceives the population must also be addressed. The following chapter proposes a method a changing this interaction through the theory of operational shock as it applies to counterinsurgency theory and identifies the characteristics of a counterinsurgency approach that achieves this affect.

Combining Concepts: Shock in Insurgencies

This section serves as the conceptual framework and describes the theory of operational shock as it applies to an insurgent organization. The section begins with a theoretical description, and concludes with a practical description of operational approaches. First, the chapter will describe the characteristics of a complex adaptive system in a state of shock. Next, the chapter will address the benefits that shocking the insurgent system provide a counterinsurgent. Finally, this chapter will identify and describe the several characteristics of a counterinsurgent's operational approach that will enable it to apply shock on an insurgent opponent.

The first thing that must be understood is that the insurgent system does not exist in a vacuum. Rather, it is simply a part of the larger societal system, as is the counterinsurgent's system.[56] Operations directed towards the insurgents have impacts on the population, just as population directed operations impact the insurgent organization. The number of actors and the

---

[56] This system consists of the population (and its own groups), the various counterinsurgent organizations, the insurgent organization, other external actors, and to a lesser degree the international community.

interactions of the insurgent systems, the counterinsurgent system, as well as the external and internal civilian systems are what make up the complexity of the environment. Shocking an insurgent system changes the nature of the interactions of all the variables.

Though complex adaptive systems are described as open systems, this is only partially true in the case of an insurgent system. Kilcullen identifies an insurgency as "energetically open but organizationally closed."[57] A mature insurgency possesses the ability to adapt to the demands of the operational environment, and in many cases dictate changes within the environment through actions of violence or exploitation of counterinsurgent mistakes. However, an insurgent system has conditions that bound and limit the "openness" of the system: the size, the communication networks available, membership qualifications, the adaptability of the leadership, the attractiveness of the cause, and ability to recruit new members. These limitations are what Kilcullen describes as the "boundaries" of the system.

These boundaries also help define the "fitness" of the system and describe the resistance of the system to shock. Dorner describes this as a "well buffered system," or one that can absorb a large amount of energy without becoming structurally unstable.[58] Basically, the more "well buffered" the organization is and the more rapidly it can assess information and distribute it to its component parts, the more resistant it is to shock. As Galula and Mao Zedong identify, an insurgency is weakest in its early stages, but it is also least likely to be seen. As the insurgency gains operational momentum, it increases its "buffering" by gaining recruits, building credibility, and establishing sanctuary areas along with building external support networks. Also, the relative strength or weakness of the environmental conditions described by Galula help frame the operational environment that strengthens or weakens the overall fitness of the insurgency. This

---

[57] Kilcullen, *Counterinsurgency,* 194.

[58] Dorner, 75.

buffering also enables the system to adapt to operational challenges and changes to the operational environment in which it operates.

As discussed earlier, a complex system operates in a state of equilibrium, a state of adaptation, or a state of chaos. In equilibrium, the system makes fewer decisions and changes less rapidly, while in chaos the system has lost control of its ability to control its adaptation. A complex adaptive system, such as an insurgency, desires to operate in a state where it can exchange energies with its environment at a pace that it can dictate, or in this "middle" state. As energies are applied against the system, it interacts with those and produces feedback and change as necessary. As the energy is increased, it is pushed towards chaos until the system creates an adaptation to counter it. The rate and type of inputs oppose the system's ability to cope, while the fitness of the system dictates how much input it could absorb.

To control a complex system, the rival must either isolate the system to push it towards equilibrium or overwhelm the system, thereby pushing it into a state of chaos. When dealing with an insurgency, it is not ideal to push it into chaos, but rather to isolate it and disaggregate it from the other actors in the operational system. A system which is operating in a state of chaos is much more unpredictable and potentially dangerous to its cohort systems until it can settle back into a non-chaotic state. A system that is driven into equilibrium, however, has the ability to make fewer decisions and adapt to its environment. It is continually isolated from its environment, forcing either a series of overreactions to regain the initiative, or the eventual irrelevance of the system.

Naveh and Boyd describe shock as increasing tension within the system and defeating (at least temporarily) the rival's rationale to fight.[59] In an insurgency, the rival system draws his

---

[59] Naveh, 258. Here, Naveh actually cites Boyd and states that "Boyd's main contribution....concerned his conception fo the operational principles of the relational manoeuvre: disruption of synergy among the elements combining the rival system.."

strength and his protection from the population. As long as the insurgent sees the population as an asset rather than as a liability, the insurgent can operate freely within it and interact in a mostly positive way with the system. This interaction enables the insurgent's narrative and continues to provide them a source of intelligence and moral strength. By denying the insurgent this asset and by changing the nature of the interaction between these actors, the counterinsurgent can increase the tension within the rival system. Increasing this internal tension, coupled with attacks against the system's structures will cause a disruption in the insurgent's ability to adapt their operational approach, providing an opportunity for the counterinsurgent to continue to inflict further damage against their cause.

To apply operational shock on an insurgent opponent, a counterinsurgency strategy must change the way in which the insurgent force sees and interacts with the population and disrupt its internal operational control mechanisms. It must isolate portions of the system through denying the insurgent's access to the population and increasing the level of tension between the operational leadership of the insurgency and the tactical executors of the strategy. Simultaneously, the counterinsurgency must overwhelm the internal structures within the system through lethal targeting and denying sanctuary. In effect, the counterinsurgent must change the cognitive terrain the insurgents occupy. Where population centric advocates focus on changing the population's perception and interaction with other members of the system, this study proposes that the counterinsurgent must focus on changing the insurgent perceptions simultaneously.

In her 2009 work, *How Terrorism Ends*, Audrey Kurth Cronin provides a framework that describes how and why terrorist campaigns end.[60] In the framework, she describes two of the

---

[60] Audrey Kurth Cronin, *How Terrorism Ends: Understanding the Decline and Demise of Terrorist Campaigns* (Princeton: Princeton University Press, 2009). The six patterns she describes that mark the end of a terrorist campaign are decapitation, negotiations, success, failure, repression, and reorientation. She also applies her framework to al-Qaeda in order to demonstrate a potential operational

variables that lead to the failure of a terror organization as the loss of operational control and fractionalization.[61] This is the essence of operational shock in an insurgency. Operational control does not imply the loss of tactical control of localized cells, but rather the inability to translate the strategic guidance of the insurgent leadership into tactical realities. It is caused by the physical and cognitive isolation of the insurgent leadership from the local actors and the disruption of the insurgent's intelligence gathering operations. Ambushes can still be conducted, new fighters can be recruited into local cells, but the linkage from the local fighter back to the strategic cause has been severed. Eventually, without this connection being reestablished, the local fighters are either taken off the battlefield or they reconcile in some way with the government forces.

Cronin describes fractionalization within a group as the individual members splintering or leaving the organization because of ideological differences or tactical disputes.[62] This fractionalization builds off of the loss of operational control within the group and often will result in increased violence between former insurgent allies. Thus, the insurgent organizations expend both energy and social capital attempting to regain control or suppress new potential rivals. The cumulative effect of this loss of control and fragmentation into disparate groups ultimately leads to the system's inability to adapt to changes within the operational environment. The disruption of the system's logic prevents the insurgency from understanding and making operational changes as feedback continues to be applied against its structures. This combination of ineffective operational guidance and inability to adapt efficiently eventually will render the insurgency operationally paralyzed until the balance can be restored.

---

approach for the United States. Though her work is focused on terror organizations, many of the organizations she analyzes are insurgencies and her model can easily be exported.

[61] Ibid., 101-103.

[62] Ibid., 100.

Operational shock on an insurgent force does not constitute a victory in a counterinsurgency campaign, just as shock within a conventional opponent can be overcome. An operational planner must not believe that by simply shocking the rival system that it will guarantee systemic collapses; there is still work to be done. Shock is a temporal effect that creates a window of opportunity to address the environmental conditions that allow the insurgency to thrive. Because the insurgency is an adaptive system, there is an opportunity for the system to regenerate once pressure is eased; or more likely, the counterinsurgent still must fully address the existing causes of instability within the operational environment. It is also not strictly enemy centric; there must be a balance of operation between efforts against the military structure of the insurgency as well as deliberate efforts to influence the population, as it will provide more options that the insurgent force must expend energies to analyze and attempt to counter.

Summary

This section explained the concept of shock within a complex system and the identified key characteristics of an insurgency in a state of shock. Complex systems often act as if they have no set rules and can confound the most experienced social scientists with their outputs. Efforts to influence and change a complex system, such as a counterinsurgency campaign, require adaptation and an approach that affects all components of the insurgent structure. The following sections are case studies of two counterinsurgency campaigns: the United States efforts in Iraq from 2006-2008 and the British campaign in Dhofar from 1965-1976. These case studies are intended to show two different expressions of this theory through two very different operational approaches and against different opponents.

CASE STUDY 1: OPERATION IRAQI FREEDOM

The United States' war in Iraq from 2003 through 2011 represents a period of immense struggle, both within the country of Iraq and for the US Army to adapt. In Iraq, the United States found a problem of a scope and scale they had not confronted in many years, perhaps ever. As rapid victory in 2003 led into the frustrations of rebuilding a nation torn apart by years of sanctions and internal conflict, the beginnings of a dynamic and lethal insurgency began to shine through. Unequipped with a coherent operational approach to deal with this rising threat, the United States spent the next three years struggling to stem the tide of violence and bring stability to Iraq.

In 2006, the US Army published Field Manual 3-24: *Counterinsurgency,* its first doctrine devoted solely to defeating insurgencies since the Cold War. The operational approaches outlined in the document, and their subsequent application in Iraq, have been described by critics as lacking in coherent strategic principles, with too much attention paid to the population centric approach.[63][64] Another criticism is that paying off former Sunni insurgents and arming a civilian militia is what stemmed the violence in Iraq. These criticisms both have some truth in their components, but represent an overly simplistic view of what was accomplished in Iraq from 2006 through 2008. This case study focuses on this period and shows that the US forces in Iraq attacked the insurgency not only through protecting the population and establishing long-term stability, but also by a deliberate attack against the structure of the insurgencies.

The Insurgency

In early 2006, the insurgency in Iraq reached its operational peak. The two primary

---

[63] Gian Gentile, "A Strategy of Tactics: Population-Centric Coin and the Army," *Parameters* (Autumn 2009): 5-17.

[64] Daniel Cox and Thomas Bruscino, introduction to *Population Centric Counterinsurgency: A False Idol?* edited by Daniel Cox and Thomas Bruscino (Ft Leavenworth, KS: Combat Studies Institute Press, 2011), 1-8.

religious sects, the Sunni and the Shia, each had separate and distinct insurgency movements battling both each other and the counterinsurgent forces of the United States and the Iraqi government. In 2004 and 2005, the violence increased each year, with major battles against Sunni insurgents in Fallujah and Shia insurgents in Najaf. Believing that the violence would decline once foreign forces left, the United States pursued a strategy of democratization and development of Iraqi security forces.[65] The Samarra mosque bombing in February 2006 pushed Iraq to a level of sectarian violence that was unheard of at that point.[66] Hundreds of Iraqis died in the ensuing months, with leaders from Al-Qaeda-in-Iraq (AQI) and Jaysh al-Mahdi (JAM) continuing to organize, equip, and recruit more fighters each month. The population, disaffected by the lack of progress promised by the United States once Saddam was out of power and appalled by the level of violence, now appeared to be looking to these insurgent organizations for protection.

The Shia insurgency was primarily led by a young cleric, Muqtada al-Sadr, through his organization, known as JAM. With a great degree of support both inside the country and from neighboring Shia dominated Iran, JAM had a sophisticated and robust, if loosely affiliated, organization. With strongholds in Basra, Karbala, Najaf, and Baghdad, JAM had a ready-made line of communication to move weapons and fighters north and south along the primary highways.[67] JAM's operational approach also included aspects similar to that of Iranian backed Hezbollah, with a large political contingent and humanitarian assistance efforts within the Shia

---

[65] Carter Malkasian, "Counterinsurgeny in Iraq: May 2003-January 2010, in *Counterinsurgency in Modern Warfare,* edited by Daniel Marston and Carter Malkasian, 287-310 (Oxford: Osprey Publishing, 2010), 302.

[66] Thomas E. Ricks, *The Gamble: General Petraeus and the American Military Adventure in Iraq,* Reprint ed. (New York: Penguin Books, 2010), 32-33.

[67] Linda Robinson, *Tell Me How This Ends: General David Petraeus and the Search for a Way Out of Iraq* (New York: PublicAffairs, 2009), 106-107.

communities.[68] In 2006, JAM controlled large areas of Baghdad through fear and intimidation, but they also served as the primary protectors of Shia from the Sunni insurgents.

The Sunni insurgency was much more disjointed and presented a series of organizations with strikingly different objectives. Organizations such as Jaysh al-Islam (JAI) and the 1920s Revolutionary Brigade represented former Baathists and Sunni nationalists who opposed the new Shia government and the American occupation of Iraq.[69] Many former Saddam-era military officers belonged to these organizations and were also aligned with the tribal structures of the Sunni areas, which created a coherent operational and governmental structure amongst the organizations. While they were dedicated to ejecting the Americans from Iraq and reasserting Sunni dominance over the Shia, these organizations could only rally limited support from within limited population groups and had little appeal to external support networks.

The catalyst for the Sunni insurgency was al-Qaeda-In-Iraq. Born from Abu Mus'ab al-Zarqawi's group, Tawhid wa'l Jihad, in 2004, AQI had accelerated the level of violence in Iraq to a new level.[70] This new organization served as a rallying point for other foreign Sunni fighters, was now at the centerpiece for Bin Laden and Zawahiri's new strategy of establishing an Islamic capitol in Baghdad.[71] AQI pulled the disparate Sunni insurgent groups under their banner and established an informal command structure with Zarqawi directing operations.[72] With the insurgent successes in Fallujah, the revelations of detainee abuse in Abu Ghirab, and the rise of

---

[68] Marisa Cochrane, *The Fragmentation of the Sadrist Movement: Iraq Report 12* (Washington DC: Institute for the Study of War, 2009).

[69] Jones, 242.

[70] Ibid., 153.

[71] Jeffrey Record, *Beating Goliath: Why Insurgencies Win* (Dulles: Potomac Books Inc., 2009), 69.

[72] Jones, 243.

JAM serving as rallying cries to the Sunni militants, Sunni dominated areas in Anbar province, Saladin province, and southwest Baghdad experienced explosive levels of violence. Driven by Zarqawi's goal of igniting a civil war within Iraq and exterminating the Shia population, AQI initiated a number of high profile attacks against the Shia population and the government.[73] However, by 2006 that same escalation of violence and subordination of other insurgent groups began to subvert the control that Zarqawi and AQI were attempting to assert on the Sunni population.

The Operational Approach

While many narratives of "the Surge" in 2007 and 2008 focus on the counterinsurgency doctrine that directly preceded it, the adaptation of the US forces in Iraq was much more complicated than additional brigades and a field manual. The prevailing idea within Multi National Force-Iraq in early 2006 was that the method to control violence was to develop the Iraqi security forces and transition the security mission to them.[74] GEN Casey, the MNF-I commander, believed that the US forces were the reason that the violence was so widespread and that by reducing the US footprint, it would bring the violence down to a level that the Iraqi's could manage. While this approach was possibly valid in early 2004, events such as Abu Ghraib and the Samarra Mosque bombing had pushed the Iraqi society to a state of chaos. There was little coordination of efforts across the country, with individual brigades and battalions determining their own approach to operations.[75] Some units were conducting traditional clear-hold-build operations while others relied on an approach of community policing and increased

---

[73] Ibid., 244-246.

[74] David Kilcullen, *The Accidental Guerrilla: Fighting Small Wars in the Midst of a Big One* (Oxford: Oxford University Press, USA, 2009), 122-128.

[75] Malkasian, 300.

lethal targeting.[76] Though an operational level headquarters, Multi National Corps- Iraq (MNC-I) existed, the their operational focus was almost solely on Baghdad itself. Operations such as Together Forward and Together Forward II were intended to quell the rising violence in Baghdad, but had little effect.[77]

In order to reestablish conditions for transfer, the US had to create a window of opportunity to grow the Iraqi security forces and solidify the Iraqi government. To reduce the violence in Iraq, the US effort had to coordinate their own efforts at the operational level and attack the insurgency at multiple levels in an effort to disrupt or dislocate them from the population. In effect, to lower the violence in the long-term, the US had to increase targeted violence in the near-term. MNC-I implemented an approach to attack the belts surrounding Baghdad, cutting off the supply routes for weapons and insurgents, while also denying AQI important sanctuary areas.[78] Understanding that any security gains would be lost without a sustained presence, the clearance operations would be done as a coordinated effort with Corps level focus, and then be followed by a sustained effort to retain the terrain seized during the clearance. Operations Phantom Thunder, Phantom Strike, and Phantom Phoenix were coordinated at the Corps level and directed against a specific set of targets, such as AQI operating in Diyala province's town of Baquba during Operation Phantom Thunder; however, they also included units remaining in the cleared areas to expand governmental control to the population.[79] Through these operations, subordinate commanders could more effectively nest their efforts into a coherent plan, providing support when necessary. This formalized operational construct also

---

[76] Kilcullen, *The Accidental Guerilla*, 124.

[77] Malkasian, 302.

[78] Ricks, 119-120.

[79] Robinson, 138-140.

provided the key enablers, such as the separate intelligence collection and development efforts, the guidance they needed to prioritize and synchronize their efforts.

This effort was complemented by a campaign by special operations forces to target and kill or capture the leadership of both AQI and JAM. Early in the campaign, the two efforts were often disjointed, as there was no friendly force to secure an area and fill the vacuum created by the elimination of a target. Most coordination was done at the tactical level between a "land owning" commander and the SOF force that was conducting the raid in their area of operations. As thousands of US forces moved in and around Baghdad to augment the existing security structure, SOF unleashed a stunning number of raids, focused mostly on destroying the AQI leadership structure.[80] As conventional forces focused on clearing insurgent strongholds and then maintaining a permanent presence, in effect attacking the horizontal structure of the insurgency, the SOF forces attacked the mid and upper level leadership of the insurgent structures. These attacks against the entire structure of the insurgency increased the tension between the leaders, who were mostly foreign fighters, and the local fighters and affiliated organizations.[81] By 2007, the coordination between the conventional and the special operations forces was no longer simply by happenstance, but rather it was a deliberate decision at the operational level.[82]

As the conventional forces and SOF attacked the military aspects of the insurgency, they also struck at the strategic depth of the problem by integrating with the diplomatic effort. Early in the campaign, units were focused on local reconstruction projects with little regard for infrastructure requirements or sustainability. These projects often left units feeling good about

---

[80] Thom Shanker, "Special Operations: High Profile, but in Shadow," *New York Times*, May 29, 2007. http://www.nytimes.com/2007/05/29/world/middleeast/29forces.html?_r=1& (accessed December 1, 2012).

[81] Jones, 255-257.

[82] Stanley A. McChrystal, *My Share of the Task: a Memoir* (New York: Portfolio Hardcover, 2013), 242.

what they had done, but did little to actually help the Iraqi people; often, the projects simply became targets for insurgents to attack because they could not be secured. Also, the integration of diplomatic and military efforts in the period prior to 2007 had been one of the limiting factors that hindered a comprehensive approach to the insurgency. In 2007, GEN Petraeus and Ambassador Ryan Crocker established a tight knit relationship, which facilitated the communication and aligned their strategic approaches.[83] At MNC-I and below, State Department representation increased and efforts were focused at the provincial level to increase the availability of services. While projects and development continued at the tactical level, they were more regulated and they connected to Iraqi institutions and were initiated with sustainability and long-term effects in mind.

Shocking the Insurgency

As discussed in the literature review section, the characteristics of an insurgency in a state of shock are a loss of operational control and a fractionalization of the organization. This disruption of cohesion within the system disrupts the logic of the insurgency and enables the counterinsurgent force to strengthen the surrounding political and social systems, setting the conditions for long-term stability. The following section describes the Sunni insurgency through these two variables, analyzing the effects of the coalition's operational approach on the insurgent structures.

Loss of Operational Control

While the elements of the Iraqi insurgency had always operated with a high degree of tactical autonomy, their increasing lethality from 2004 to 2006 was due to their ability to coordinate amongst their tactical groups. Zawahiri's strategic guidance to Zarqawi, the

---

[83] Ricks, 139.

operational level commander, was to expel the United States from Iraq in order to set the conditions for the establishment of an Islamic Caliphate. Zarqawi transferred this strategic intent and created an operational approach that consisted of uniting the Sunni insurgent groups under one banner, creating a belief that AQI was the only organization that could protect the Sunni from the Shia, and lastly igniting a civil war in order to discredit both the coalition and the Iraqi government. His operational plan was to control the "belts" which surround Baghdad, enabling his commanders to move supplies and fighters in and out of the city.[84] His concept sketch for this campaign plan was found on his body after he was killed by an airstrike in June 2006.[85]

The coalition disrupted AQI's ability to exercise operational control in two ways. First was through their campaign of targeted raids against AQI mid and senior level operatives. The effects of these raids were three-fold. First, and most obviously, it took leaders off the battlefield, forcing the organization to promote from within and causing friction within the network. Second, many of the raids resulted in large amounts of intelligence, which SOF and coalition forces became increasingly capable of analyzing and following rapidly onto another target. The speed and frequency of these targeted attacks against multiple echelons of leadership became increasingly difficult for AQI to recover from.[86] The third, and possibly most important, effect was that the raids forced leaders such as Zarqawi to take great precautions in their movements and their communications. This disrupted their ability to both receive strategic guidance and to update their subordinates to changes in the operational plan.

The second effort of the coalition to undermine the operational control of the insurgency

---

[84] McChrystal, *My Share of the Task*, 189.

[85] Bill Roggio, "Iraqi Troops Kill Senior Al Qaeda in Iraq Leader," *Long War Journal* (Nov 7, 2008): http://www.longwarjournal.org/archives/2008/11/iraqi_troops_kill_se.php (accessed February 1, 2013.

[86] McChrystal, *My Share of the Task*, 154.

was their effort to attack the belts that Zarqawi had identified on his concept sketch. Following Kalyvas' theory of applying selective violence and contesting the insurgency for control, MNC-I's Phantom-series operations drove senior and mid level leaders out of historic safe havens such as Baquba, and then the persistent presence in the area made reintegration for those leaders much more difficult.[87] As Kalyvas identifies, with control of an area comes collaboration, and when coalition forces proved that they were staying in an area, the amount of collaboration with the population increased. This enabled further targeting, both by SOF and conventional forces, against the leadership that remained in the area.[88] Through their selective application of clearance operations and raids, the coalition was able to inject enough energy into the enemy system to isolate the insurgent leadership from the population rather than push the area into a state of chaos. With no guidance from higher-level commanders, many fighters eventually chose to simply stop fighting until operational level leadership returned, while others joined with coalition forces and reconciled, at least outwardly, with the Iraqi government.

Fractionalization

As stated earlier, AQI served as a critical link for numerous Sunni insurgent groups with differing objectives. Through AQI, groups such as JAI and the 1920s Revolutionary Brigade could draw support and funds from external sources that they would not ordinarily have access to. However, throughout the course of the campaign, several of these groups broke away and many joined sides with the coalition. The coalition's operational approach encouraged this fractionalization through an aggressive targeting of senior and mid level AQI leadership and through providing the less extreme of the elements an opportunity to break away through reconciliation programs and increasing opportunities for collaboration.

---

[87] Kilcullen, *The Accidental Guerilla*, 144-145.

[88] Ibid., 147.

While the extreme nature of AQI's treatment of local Iraqi's was one of the main factors in this fragmentation, the loss of terrain and the ability to execute control over their subordinates also enabled other organizations to break away. As AQI leaders were targeted at an increasing rate and their ability to control and influence the Sunni population declined, they turned to more violent methods of coercion. This violence, coupled with the increased access of the coalition forces, enabled the less ideologically aligned groups within the Sunni insurgency to make a choice and leave the alliance. While some critics argue that the increase of forces and the effort to secure the population had little effect on the overall outcome of the campaign, the coalition would not have been in a position to give the groups that choice had it not been for the change in approach.

AQI's Sunni confederation also began to fall apart as the surrounding systems, notably the military forces sent to secure areas and the Iraqi government, began to grow in capability, or stated another way, became more buffered. Having essentially boycotted the 2005 elections, the Sunni population began to understand in late 2006 that the road to peace in their country did not run through AQI, but rather through engaging the growing central government. The most popular of the tribal uprisings occurred in Anbar Province with Sheik Sitar and the Abu Risha clan; however, AQI's alliances throughout western Iraq began to wane throughout 2006 and into 2007. In Zaidon, a district south west of Baghdad, members of the 1920s Brigade, a group of former regime loyalists who had aligned themselves under AQI's banner for several years, approached coalition leaders looking to partner with them against AQI. The combination of lethal targeting by the Marine unit and ongoing disputes with AQI had damaged the organization to the point where they chose to align with the coalition rather than continue to work with the extremists.[89]

---

[89] Ibid., 163.

Summary

The cumulative effect of the operational adaptations made by the US forces and the coordination between the various elements of the US counterinsurgency effort effectively fragmented the Sunni insurgencies and severely degraded AQI's operational capabilities. Following Zarqawi's death, AQI's new leader, Abu Ayyub al-Masri, was effectively cognitively and physically isolated from his Sunni recruiting base because of the amount of pressure from JSOC elements, until his death in 2010. While al-Qaeda in Iraq never fully dissolved, they never regained the same operational footing or capability that they had at their operational peak in 2006.

Despite an initial spike in violence during the beginning stages of the operation, casualty numbers drastically declined throughout late 2007 and into 2008. The levels of violence, either against the coalition or against the Iraqi population, never returned to the levels of 2005-2006. The resulting decline enabled both the Iraqi Army and the Iraqi government to further refine their capabilities and grow in size, setting the conditions for the transition of security responsibilities.

CASE STUDY 2: DHOFAR 1965-1976

In 1965, the British Army was quite familiar with the type of war they were about to

enter into in Oman. Since the end of the Second World War, Great Britain had fought a number

of insurgencies throughout their former colonies; including Malaya, Cyprus, and a separate

campaign just ten years prior in Oman. The British model for counterinsurgency, labeled in

many circles as "winning hearts and minds," had been effective in dealing with these small wars.

Situated alongside the Strait of Hormuz, a major oil-shipping lane, the internal security of

Oman remained an area of concern for Western powers, most notably the British.[90] Allies since

their first treaty was signed in 1798, the British had a long history of coming to the aid of the

Sultanate in times of both internal and external threats.[91] British officers served as advisors, and

in many cases commanders, to the Omani military forces. The Sultan's own son attended the

British military academy at Sandhurst. As the military situation on the ground worsened, it was

only natural for the Sultan to reach out to his British counterparts for assistance.

The insurgency in Dhofar from 1965 to 1976 represented a hard test of the British way of

counterinsurgency as well as a turning point in the relationship between Britain and Oman. The

first five years of the campaign represent a period of abject failure for the governmental forces.

However, in 1970, the government staged a stunning turn of events and regained its momentum,

eventually resulting in a resounding victory against the insurgents. Enabled by a focused military

campaign and complimented by necessary changes within the political situation, the government

retook control of the Dhofar region from the insurgency and stabilized the country. This case

---

[90] Ian Beckett, "The British Counter-insurgency Campaign in Dhofar, 1965-1975," in *Counterinsurgency in Modern Warfare,* edited by Daniel Marston and Carter Malkasian 175-190 (Oxford: Osprey Publishing, 2010), 175.

[91] John McKeown, "Britain and Oman: The Dhofar War and Its Significance" (PhD diss., University of Cambridge, 1981), 6.

study examines the changes in the British and Omani operational approach and their effects on the insurgency that led to a decisive victory.

The Insurgency

The insurgency in Dhofar was, to a large extent, one of the government's own making. The Sultan in 1965, Sa'id bin Taymur, was an isolationist who had been in power for over thirty years and. There were only three state run schools and only one hospital, which was run through external funding. He attempted to keep all external influences away from his population in the fear that it would corrupt them.[92] People were not allowed to move around the country without permission, while the Sultan himself remained mostly shuttered inside his home.[93] The population in Dhofar, a governate that bordered Yemen and the furthest from the capital in Muscat, felt increasingly isolated from the rest of the country. The rest of the population began to become desperate for some sort of change that would enable them to gain access to the modernization that the rest of the world was experiencing. The citizens of Oman, and particularly Dhofar, were fraught with dissatisfaction and were looking for a change.

Neighboring Yemen presented a possibility for change. Arab Marxists, backed by the USSR, China, and Egypt won control of the country in 1967 and were looking to expand their revolution into new lands.[94] This group, which would become the Dhofar Liberation Front (DLF), found a loose confederation of groups within Dhofar all seeking different objectives and with no unifying purpose or cause to unite them. The groups came together in 1965 to air their

---

[92] Jim White, "Oman 1965-1976: From Certain Defeat to Decisive Victory," *Small Wars Journal* (1 Sept 2008): 4, http://smallwarsjournal.com/mag/docs-temp/93-white.pdf (accessed February 1, 2013).

[93] Beckett, 176.

[94] Richard Belfield and Roger Cole, *SAS Operation Storm: Nine Men Against Four Hundred*, Reprint ed. (London: Hodder & Stoughton, 2012), 22.

43

complaints and determine a course of action to achieve their initial objectives. The tribes of

Dhofar wanted liberation from an oppressive regime, the communists saw an opportunity to

spread their ideology, and Egypt saw another way to eject British influence from the peninsula.[95]

Initial operations by the DLF from 1965 through 1966 were moderately successful, but mostly

because of the ineffective and half-hearted response by the government forces.[96] By 1967,

Yemen was a Marxist regime, which provided a sanctuary beyond the reach of the Sultan's

Armed Forces (SAF), and the communists had seized control of the insurgency. All the groups,

which had originated as disparate organizations with very different goals, now merged under the

umbrella of one organization, the Popular Front for the Liberation of the Occupied Arabian Gulf

(PFLOAG).[97]

The formation of the PFLOAG altered the nature of the insurgency and changed the

dynamics of the insurgent system. Armed with a guiding logic of communism, the insurgency

now had not only a cause to drive it forward, but it had a time tested operational approach to

implement. This change also provided the insurgents connection to large amounts of external

support, through other communist nations, that it had not enjoyed before. As the SAF attempted

to combat the insurgency with minimal forces and by isolating the Dhofar region, the PFLOAG

grew to over 2,000 full-time fighters, with almost 3,000 part-time militia filling out their ranks.[98]

However, along with the support and this expertise came expectations. The Marxists

instituted a strict indoctrination program, enrolling children in their programs and forcing them to

---

[95] Ibid., 23.

[96] Beckett, 178.

[97] White, 5.

[98] McKeown, 45

renounce Islam.[99] This created an immediate weakness in the operational structure of the insurgency, as it required the leadership to completely change the logic of the population they sought to recruit. Islam was not only their religion, but it was the way of life for the extremely poor but devout Dhofari people. To enforce this change and attempt to eliminate this weakness, the PFLOAG established death squads known as *idaarat* to intimidated the unwilling into remaining passive supporters of the movement.[100] These death squads, many led by Dhofaris who had been sent away to indoctrination in the Soviet Union or China, were ruthless in their enforcement of communist ideology, focusing their attacks on the tribal leaders who did not conform.[101] By focusing their energies against both the religion and the tribal structure, the communists were attempting to neutralize two of the pillars of Dhofari life and to create a new power structure. These efforts, while they enabled short-term successes, would eventually turn on them.

Despite these affronts to the basic power structures of the Dhofari people, the insurgency continued to grow and had great success in the early phases of the campaign. By 1970, the SAF only controlled three of towns within the Dhofar region and their ability to move was severely limited.[102] The government's heavy-handed approach and indiscriminate use of force, coupled with their inability to control any territory further pushed the population into the arms of the insurgency by providing them no realistic alternative.[103]

---

[99] Belfield, 25.

[100] Beckett, 178.

[101] Belfield, 47.

[102] Beckett, 178.

[103] White, 5.

The Operational Approach

The operational approach for the campaign is divided into two distinct phases. The first phase, from 1965 through 1970, was marred by a series of defeats for the government. Focusing almost entirely on a military line of effort, the SAF, which numbered less that 1,000 at the outset of hostilities, originally attempted to suppress the entire population and treated all Dhofaris as potential enemies.[104] The SAF continued to upgrade their equipment and increase troop levels, but without the ability to acquire accurate intelligence, target enemy locations, and provide the citizens of Dhofar any alternative to supporting the insurgency, they were continually met with failure.

Not only was there no real non-lethal component to the campaign plan, the government actually took actions to deliberately target the population. The Sultan banned all Dhofaris from the Armed Forces and essentially treated the operations in Dhofar as an occupation. The city of Salalah was encircled in wire and the movements of the population were severely restricted.[105] The SAF would shell populated areas before conducting clearance operations, conduct indiscriminate attacks against civilian's homes, and would often not stay and hold any of the territory they had just cleared.[106] These attacks against the population placed the people of Dhofar in an inescapable situation; they had a group of communists who lived amongst them and would kill them if they did not support them, and they had a government who believed they were a threat and would kill them for not supporting them.

However, in 1970, a change in strategic leadership enabled the necessary changes in the

---

[104] Jacqueline Hazelton, "Compellence and Accommodation in Counterinsurgency Warfare" (diss., Brandeis University, 2011), 66.

[105] White, 5.

[106] Hazelton, 68.

operational approach. On July 23, 1970, the Sandhurst-educated son of the Sultan, Qaboos bin Said, led a coup that deposed his father's regime. Qaboos instituted immediate changes at both the political level and in the military approach. First, he grew his security forces from 3,800 in 1970 to over 18,000 by 1975.[107] He also lifted restrictions on movement inside the country and announced a series of development projects that appealed to the needs of his people.[108] He also, in a move that resounded throughout the insurgent structure, offered amnesty to fighters who wished to put down their arms.[109] The National Defense Council was established in 1972, as there was little existing governmental structure to unify and control the efforts of the campaign.[110] External support from Iran, Jordan, and Saudi Arabia also came after Qaboos took power.[111] These strategic level reforms enabled the government to confront the strategic depth of the insurgency, addressing many of the preexisting environmental conditions that allowed for its growth.

Operationally, the SAF and their British Special Air Service (SAS) advisors also changed the way they prosecuted the campaign. This campaign emphasized a balanced non-lethal aspect to attempt and coerce the Dhofaris to reject the Marxist influence. Civic Action Teams (CATs) were organized and employed throughout the campaign following the clearance of an area to show the government's presence and their commitment.[112] This is not to infer that the approach was strictly non-lethal. The governmental forces adopted an approach similar to clear-hold-build

---

[107] Ibid., 75.

[108] Beckett, 179.

[109] McKeown, 50.

[110] Beckett, 180.

[111] Hazelton, 76.

[112] Bard O'Neill, "Revolutionary War in Oman" in *Insurgency in the Modern World,* edited by Bard O'Neill. (Boulder, Colorado: Westview Press, 1980), 225.

and they conducted air and ground assaults against enemy strongpoints and supply lines to directly target the insurgent's military capability.[113] Through following these clearance operations with a security force, the SAF could build collaboration and cooperation from the locals, though often not full commitment.[114] During this stage of the campaign it was not important that the population fully supported the government, but what was important is that their ability to connect with and be influenced by the insurgents was disrupted.

The SAS also started a deliberate initiative to create and develop intelligence collection teams based around signals intelligence and co-opted rebel fighters that were organized into militia formations known as *firqats*.[115] This increased intelligence flow not only enabled better targeting of PLOAG leadership, but it also increased the government's understanding of the PLOAG's operational structure.[116] This information enabled the government to target the cognitive and emotional tension that the Marxists were creating inside of their own organization: the requirement to do away with tribalism and Islam to be a part of the organization. This tension became the focus of the governmental information campaign, transmitted through word of mouth, leaflets, and radio broadcasts.[117]

Shocking the Insurgency

Unlike the Iraqi insurgency, the PLOAG eventually imploded. However, this did not happen overnight. While held up as a shining example of population centric counterinsurgency, many of the reforms that the new government proposed and broadcast did not go into effect until

---

[113] Ibid., 226.

[114] Hazelton, 87.

[115] Ibid., 77.

[116] Beckett, 182.

[117] Ibid., 183.

well after the insurgency was defeated. This section examines the effects of the government's operations and how they denied the insurgency the ability to effectively control their elements, which led to the eventual fractionalization of the movement.

Loss of Operational Control

For the first five years of the campaign, the PFLOAG continuously consolidated control of the movement. By late 1970, the PFLOAG had effectively assumed operational control from the entire insurgency in Dhofar and had suppressed all the former nationalist elements within the movement. They were also winning the campaign. The military wing of the movement, the People's Liberation Army (PLA), controlled the lines of communication throughout Dhofar and maintained supply lines back into Yemen, where the majority of their external support came from. This freedom of movement enabled the PFLOAG leadership to coordinate attacks, transport fighters, and issue guidance for lethal and non-lethal operations. The insurgency was able to fight within its capabilities because it retained the key terrain and the initiative.[118]

With the change in operational approach, the SAF increased the pressure on the PFLOAG, both by challenging them for territory and by interdicting their lines of communication. In 1971, Operations Leopard, Puma, and Cougar all targeted the insurgency's ability to conduct resupply.[119] Destroying the insurgency's caches and choking them off of supplies left local commanders to fend for themselves, both for weapons and for food. This increasing sense of desperation led to an ill-advised attack against a government stronghold in Mirbat, which resulted in a decisive defeat, both physically and psychologically, for the insurgency.[120]

---

[118] Belfield, 63.

[119] Hazelton, 89.

[120] Belfield, 251.

49

Furthermore, the increased presence of governmental forces and the integration of former fighters into the militia made the movement of leadership much more difficult. Because of this disruption, and the increasing dissatisfaction of local Dhofaris with the insurgency, a movement to allow for greater autonomy at the lower levels was instituted; however, this initiative was largely ineffective.[121]

Fractionalization

As stated earlier in the case study, the seeds of disaggregation were present within the insurgency from the very beginning. This new insurgent system was not something that arose from a natural condition within that social network, but rather it was formed by the interaction of two foreign entities. The PFLOAG underestimated how ingrained Islam was into the Dhofari way of life and ignored both the tendency and the potential of the existing social system. This emergent system revealed an organization that was unified only in hatred of the government, but asymmetric in their long-term objectives. As the government gathered intelligence and revealed the weakness of the emerging network, they exploited this rift and created a disruption in the logic of the new system. Because of the weakness of the enemy network, the friendly forces did not have to create meaningful changes; they simply had to show the desire to make some changes while allowing the Dhofari system to return to the pillars of their previous condition.

Though the military operations of the campaign focused on attacking the insurgency while not alienating the population, it was the social and political movements of the government that had the greatest effect on the insurgency's structures. The military's role was to maintain pressure on the insurgency and force them into attempting to compel the population through acts of violence, which they had the propensity to do anyways, and then to deny the insurgency access to that population while the government issued its message.

---

[121] McKeown, 83.

The policy of amnesty for the rebel fighters also had a jarring impact on the insurgency. A large number of fighers opted to come over to the government's side from 1970-1975, many joining the SAS-trained *firqats* and choosing to fight against the communists.[122] Amnesty also provided the nationalists who joined up originally to gain concessions from the government a mechanism to stop fighting.[123] The widespread defections led the PFLOAG to change its name to the Popular Front for the Liberation of Oman (PFLO) in 1974, in an attempt to bring a more local logic to the operation.[124] However, by this point the rebellion was in full retreat, with external support waning and freedom of movement internally now severely limited.

Summary

The British campaign in Dhofar has been held up as a classic example of a population-centric campaign by some analysts, while the veracity of those claims have been challenged in recent years.[125] It does, however, represent a campaign in which the counterinsurgent created a massive change within the operational environment that disrupted the organizing logic of the insurgency it faced. The space created by the successful campaign not only allowed for Sultan Qaboos to enact further reforms after the insurgency was defeated, but it also protected a strategic chokepoint of the world's oil. The networked approach of the counterinsurgents and their ability to adapt their operational approach once they determined the nature of the threat enabled the SAS and the Omani government to attack the insurgency across the breadth and depth of their structures, eventually causing a complete collapse of the organization.

---

[122] White, 7.

[123] McKeown, 55.

[124] Ibid., 83.

[125] The author is referring to Dr. Ian Beckett and Jim White as being in the "pro" population centric court, with Dr. Hazelton arguing that the tenets of population centric counterinsurgency, namely true governmental reform and protection of the population were not enacted during the campaign.

CONCLUSION

This paper examined the concept of operational shock and applied it in the context of a counterinsurgency campaign. Though never explicitly stated, operational shock is at the heart of the US Army's current doctrine.[126] This study's intention was to connect the concepts found in current US Army operational doctrine with those that exist currently within the counterinsurgency lexicon in an effort to provide a mental model for an operational planner. Complexity science provided the intellectual framework upon which the rest of the work is based, using the assumption that an insurgency represents a complex adaptive system. Finally, the study examined two historical campaigns, using the characteristics of a system in a state of shock to analyze the effects that the counterinsurgent's operational approach had on their respective opponents.

The campaigns in Iraq and Dhofar show that it is possible to affect an insurgency at the operational level through different approaches and with different force structures. Though the historical time frame, strategic aims, and types of insurgencies differ, there are many commonalities between the two campaigns. This conclusion will examine the traits of the operational approaches that enabled the British and the United States to operationally shock their respective opponents and it will make recommendations for further research.

Key Characteristics

Networked Approach

GEN Stanley McChrystal, the former commander of both the Joint Special Operations Command (JSOC) and International Security Assistance Force (ISAF) described fighting a

---

[126] ADP 3-0, 2-2. Paragraph 2-5 states that the goal of commanders is to force the enemy to respond to our actions and "never recover from initial shock of the attack." It goes on to discuss that the goal is to not only destroy enemy weapons and equipment, but to render the opponent unable to make coherent operational decisions and abandon preferred courses of action. These statements encapsulate what Isserson and Naveh are trying to achieve through their deep attacks and fractionalization strikes.

modern day insurgency as fighting a network within a network.[127] This approach is focused on incorporating all the components of the counterinsurgency efforts in an effort to effectively "flatten" the organization and spread information laterally as well as vertically. This is not simply the "whole of government" approach, but rather a deliberate effort to coordinate efforts at the operational level. This network must include all the lethal and nonlethal efforts, special operations and conventional forces, as well as the international diplomatic efforts with the localized development projects.

FM 3-24 refers to aspects of networking as "unity of effort," which emphasizes the primacy of focusing both the political and the military aspects of the campaign. The manual also calls for a single commander of the counterinsurgency effort.[128] However, the modern reality is that there will rarely be a unified commander of a complete effort, and that there will be a number of actors, but underneath and outside of the traditional lines of control. To truly create an effort that is collaborative and therefore able to understand the multiple structures within the operational environment, the counterinsurgent force must establish a force structure which allows for rapid information acquisition, analysis, and dissemination.

Through the integration of these efforts, the counterinsurgent effectively "buffers" the systems that surround the insurgency. This is the difference between pushing the insurgency into a state of shock and sending the insurgency, and potentially the entire system, into chaos. Strengthening the political structures and the security forces of the counterinsurgents and connecting those efforts to the local population strengthens the links between those systems and protects them from the insurgency as energy is applied against it. Despite the early efforts of

---

[127] Stanley McChrystal, "It Takes a Network," *Foreign Policy*, March/April 2011, http://www.foreignpolicy.com/articles/2011/02/22/it_takes_a_network?page=0,2 (accessed December 3, 2012).

[128] FM 3-24, 1-22.

commanders in Iraq to build the Iraqi security forces, the weakness of both the Iraqi government and their connection to the people only increased the rates of violence as the coalition forces targeted the insurgents.

Integrating all the efforts allows the counterinsurgent to attack the entire structure of the insurgent organization simultaneously. Naveh describes a "horizontal" and a "vertical" structure within a military system; the horizontal structure has the capacity to absorb the energy from a rival while the vertical structures retain the system's ability to deliver a blow.[129] In an irregular system, the lower level insurgents and fighters represent this horizontal structure while the insurgent leadership represents the vertical structure. While some authors have argued that the population represents the operational depth of the insurgency, this study proposes that the mid and upper level leadership is the true operational depth, with the population representing a strategic requirement for the insurgency.[130] By integrating conventional efforts with the special operations efforts, it enables targeting across all the structures of the insurgent organization. The long-term diplomatic and development efforts shape the operational environment, attack the strategic depth of the insurgency, and set the conditions for long-term success. However, these efforts must also be nested with the operational actions of the counterinsurgent's military forces in order to achieve their maximum effect.

The term "networked" can infer that this is a modernized approach with sophisticated communications equipment, but this is not the case. In the Dhofar campaign, the centralization of the political and military structure effectively networked the efforts of the entire counterinsurgentcy effort and provided the buffering needed to protect the system. The creation

---

[129] Naveh, 17.

[130] Lee Grubbs and Michael Forsyth, "Is There a Deep Fight in Counterinsurgency?" *Military Review* (July-August 2005): 28-31, http://www.au.af.mil/au/awc/awcgate/milreview/grubbs.pdf (accessed December 3, 2012).

of both the defense council and the development council by Sultan Qaboos created a unity of effort and focused the energies of the organization on defeating the insurgents. While the ability to execute precision targets against enemy leadership was not as refined as it is in the modern context, the integration of the intelligence collection effort into the operational effort enabled the government to capitalize on the strategic weakness of the insurgency: the fundamental disconnect between the Marxist ideology and the Dhofari attachment to tribe and religion.

Adaptation

The current U.S. strategic defense guidance states that while the United States will retain the capability to act across the full range of military operations, they will not be organized or equipped to conduct long-term counterinsurgency operations. This would lead planners to look for one of a few approaches: either avoid insurgencies or threats like them all together or find a faster way to defeat them. Unfortunately, history does not indicate that there are any quick fixes to insurgent networks. Additional study of complexity theory also indicates that when encountering a complex system such as an insurgent organization, it takes time to understand and interpret the actions of the organization. Taking decisive action against an irregular system without an understanding of its nature and the nature of the interactions within the system can have catastrophic consequences.[131]

No matter how much cultural understanding or intelligence preparation a unit does, complexity science shows why early success is so difficult to achieve in counterinsurgency. An analyst can understand the dynamics of an indigenous population, but they cannot fully understand how that system will react when the counterinsurgent force interacts with it. Only after allowing the two systems to interact can the analyst begin to understand the nature of the

---

[131] This is the central thesis of Dorner's work in *The Logic of Failure*. He presents numerous examples of "experts" who make seemingly logical decisions early in a computer simulation. However, because these experts do not fully understand the impact of their decisions on the system, these early successes eventually resulted in new catastrophes from which they could not recover.

interaction and predict how to dictate reactions within them. In Iraq, despite criticisms that the United States should have had a more refined plan to combat the insurgency from the outset, the insurgency evolved and changed over time. The insurgency was not the same in 2006 as it was in 2004. It took time before planners could understand how the system would react as certain stimuli were applied to it. It also took time for the surrounding Iraqi social system to take in the introduction of al-Qaeda and their ideology and process it before that system could reject it.

The counterinsurgent organization must develop systems that enable it to access and adjust to changes within the environment. In Dhofar, the creation of the militias enabled a greater degree of intelligence collection, which enabled them to exploit the insurgent weaknesses. Essentially, as Dorner states, the counterinsurgent organization must formulate a hypothesis and then test it. The early operational approach must be deliberately open in order to allow for this organizational learning. However, once a level of operational understanding has been achieved, the organization must be able to rapidly adjust its operational approach to affect the insurgent system systemically. Only by understanding the cultural context, the nature of the insurgency, and the potential of the friendly system can the counterinsurgent make a realistic and operationally viable plan for attacking and defeating the insurgent system.

Selective Violence in Contested Spaces

Despite the cognitive and emotional nature of counterinsurgency, terrain still matters in the context of a counterinsurgency campaign. Creating rapid change in the operational environment, coupled with the attacks across the breadth and depth of the insurgent structures changes the insurgent's perception of the environment. These changes and the attacks force the insurgent system to expend energies to learn and to adapt, while also trying to survive. The insurgency requires areas that it can regenerate combat power and the space to make decisions without the threat of attack. In order to deny the insurgents this asset and maintain operational pressure, the counterinsurgent must increase the number of contested areas, while maintaining the selective application of violence against the insurgent structure. Through this continuous application of pressure and the requirement of the insurgency to expend energies to cope with all these factors, the counterinsurgent will push the insurgent system beyond its ability to make coherent operational adaptations, effectively placing it in a state of shock.

Contesting areas of control also forces the insurgency to interact with the population differently. If the insurgent is unopposed in an area, the population is seen as an asset they can exploit with relative impunity. However, when the counterinsurgent contests the insurgent for control of that area, the insurgents must now look at the population as a potential liability, changing the nature of that interaction. In both Dhofar and Iraq, the counterinsurgents began to see lasting results when they began to conduct sustained operations to challenge their respective insurgencies for control. When the SAF changed their approach in 1971 and began challenging the insurgency for terrain, the insurgency had to change the way they moved in and amongst the population. As Kalyvas identifies, in areas of contested control, the population will side with the group that exerts violence in the most selective way possible.[132] This application of violence and the control that comes with it enables the further collection of intelligence, enabling the counterinsurgent to increase their lethality and selectivity. This collaboration creates tension within the insurgent system, forcing them to either retreat from the area or try to intimidate the population from collaborating. Thus, the protection of civilians and the avoidance of civilian casualties becomes not only a legal requirement, but it is an operational requirement for success.

While denying the enemy access to the population is key, the counterinsurgent must not overcommit their forces and attempt to contest too many areas. The MNC-I operations in 2007-2008 were designed to ensure that the coalition forces could target and seize terrain, while still retaining the necessary force structure to react to changes. If this is not done, the

---

[132] Kalyvas, 173.

counterinsurgent will be unable to match the insurgent's ability to influence the population and the counterinsurgent's ability to target effectively will be lessened.[133] The counterinsurgent force must select these targeted areas carefully and then apply their forces against them. The counterinsurgent can spread its influence through other factors such as economic impact and information operations, but to effectively control an area and change the fundamental nature of the interactions, security forces must be applied. Through this effective use of violence in selected areas, the counterinsurgent can change both the physical and the cognitive terrain that the insurgents operate within, further stressing the system.

Recommendations for Further Research

Much has been written about the application of operational art in the context of a counterinsurgency campaign, however little is written about shock in insurgencies. An additional area of research should examine the characteristics of an insurgency that would make it resistant to shock, and what modifications to an operational approach would be needed in order to overcome that resistance. Also, with the increased emphasis of organizations such as Human Terrain Systems in counterinsurgency operations, what is their actual impact in enabling operational adaptation vice simply increasing tactical understanding? Finally, how will the Army's current shift towards Regionally Aligned Brigades impact on their ability to understand, network, and adapt more rapidly when faced with an insurgency in a partner nation?

Closing

This monograph did not set out to disprove counterinsurgent theory nor did it intend to create a new one, but simply to provide a conceptualization of a counterinsurgency campaign through a different lens. The creation of FM 3-24 in 2006 represented an intellectual turning

---

[133] This is an additional illustration of Kalyvas' five areas of control.

point for much of the Army and has been the subject of much debate. The document was necessary at the time it was written and there is much that the manual can teach the force. Unfortunately, it enabled a degree of intellectual laziness in that it led its readers to believe that if they simply focused on the conditions surrounding the insurgency, it would simply go away. The population represents the prize in a counterinsurgency campaign, but not always the center of gravity.

BIBLIOGRAPHY

Books and Articles

Adamsky, Dima. *The Culture of Military Innovation: the Impact of Cultural Factors On the Revolution in Military Affairs in Russia, the US, and Israel.* Stanford, Calif.: Stanford Security Studies, 2010.

Beckett, Ian. "The British Counter-insurgency Campaign in Dhofar, 1965-1975." In *Counterinsurgency in Modern Warfare,* edited by Daniel Marston and Carter Malkasian, 175-190. Oxford: Osprey Publishing, 2010.

Bousquet, Antoine J. *The Scientific Way of Warfare: Order and Chaos On the Battlefields of Modernity.* New York, NY: Columbia University Press, 2010.

Belfield, Richard, and Roger Cole. *Sas Operation Storm: Nine Men Against Four Hundred.* Reprint ed. London: Hodder & Stoughton, 2012.

Cochrane Marisa. *The Fragmentation of the Sadrist Movement: Iraq Report 12.* Washington DC: Institute for the Study of War, 2009.

Cox, Daniel and Thomas Bruscino. Introduction to *Population Centric Counterinsurgency: A False Idol?* edited by Daniel Cox and Thomas Bruscino, 1-8. Ft Leavenworth, KS: Combat Studies Institute Press, 2011.

Cronin, Audrey Kurth. *How Terrorism Ends: Understanding the Decline and Demise of Terrorist Campaigns.* Princeton: Princeton University Press, 2009.

Dorner, Dietrich. *The Logic of Failure: Recognizing and Avoiding Error in Complex Situations.* Reading, Mass.: Basic Books, 1997.

Galula, David. *Counterinsurgency Warfare: Theory and Practice* .Saint Petersburg, FL: Glenwood Press, 1964.

Gentile, Gian. "A Strategy of Tactics: Population-Centric Coin and the Army." *Parameters* (Autumn 2009).

Gharajedaghi, Jamshid. *Systems Thinking: Managing Chaos and Complexity: a Platform for Designing Business Architecture.* 2nd ed. Boston, MA: Butterworth-Heinemann, 2006.

Hammes, Thomas X. Hammes. *The Sling and the Stone: On War in the 21st Century.* Mechanicsburg, PA: Zenith Press, 2006.

Isserson, G.S. *"The Evolution of Operational Art."* Translated by Bruce W. Menning. Fort Leavenworth, KS: SAMS Theoretical Special Edition, 2005.

Johnson, Neil. *Simply Complexity.* Oxford, England: Oneworld Publications, 2009.

Jones, Seth G. *Hunting in the Shadows: the Pursuit of Al Qa'ida Since 9/11*. New York: W. W. Norton & Company, 2012.

Kalyvas, Stathis N. *The Logic of Violence in Civil War*. NEW YORK: Cambridge University Press, 2006.

Kilcullen, David. *Counterinsurgency*. Oxford: Oxford University Press, USA, 2010.

Kilcullen, David. *The Accidental Guerrilla: Fighting Small Wars in the Midst of a Big One*. Oxford: Oxford University Press, 2009.

Laszlo, Alexander and Stanley Krippner. *Systems Theories: Their Origins, Foundations, and Development*. In *Systems Theories and A Priori Aspects of Perception*, edited by J.S. Jordan, 47-74. Amsterdam: Elsevier Science, 1998.

Malkasian, Carter. "Counterinsurgency in Iraq: May 2003-January 2010." In *Counterinsurgency in Modern Warfare*, edited by Daniel Marston and Carter Malkasian, 287-310. Oxford: Osprey Publishing, 2010.

Matthews, Matt M. *We Were Caught Unprepared: The 2006 Hezbollah-Israeli War*. Leavenworth, KS, 2008.

McChrystal, Stanley. *My Share of the Task: a Memoir*. New York: Portfolio Hardcover, 2013.

Murray, Williamson, and Peter R. Mansoor, eds. *Hybrid Warfare*. New York: Cambridge University Press, 2012.

Naveh, Shimon. *In Pursuit of Military Excellence: the Evolution of Operational Theory*. London: Routledge, 1997.

O'Neill, Bard E. *Insurgency & Terrorism: from Revolution to Apocalypse*. 2nd ed. Washington, D.C.: Potomac Books Inc., 2005.

O'Neill, Bard. "Revolutionary War in Oman." In *Insurgency in the Modern World*, edited by Bard O'Neill, 213-233. Boulder, Colorado: Westview Press, 1980.

Osinga, Frans P.B. *Science, Strategy and War: the Strategic Theory of John Boyd*. London: Routledge, 2006.

Record, Jeffrey. *Beating Goliath: Why Insurgencies Win*. Dulles: Potomac Books Inc., 2007.

Ricks, Thomas E. *The Gamble: General David Petraeus and the American Military Adventure in Iraq, 2006-2008*. New York: Penguin Press HC, The, 2009.

Robinson, Linda. *Tell Me How This Ends: General David Petraeus and the Search for a Way Out of Iraq*. New York: PublicAffairs, 2009.

Dissertations

Hazelton, Jacqueline. "Compellence and Accommodation in Counterinsurgency Warfare." diss., Brandeis University, 2011.

McKeown, John. "Britain and Oman: The Dhofar War and Its Significance." diss., University of Cambridge, 1981.

Online Sources

Grubbs, Lee and Michael Forsyth, "Is There a Deep Fight in Counterinsurgency?" *Military Review* (July-August 2005): 28-31, http://www.au.af.mil/au/awc/awcgate/milreview/grubbs.pdf (accessed December 3, 2012).

McChrystal, Stanley. "It Takes a Network," *Foreign Policy*, March/April 2011, http://www.foreignpolicy.com/articles/2011/02/22/it_takes_a_network?page=0,2 (accessed December 3, 2012).

Roggio, Bill. "Iraqi Troops Kill Senior Al Qaeda in Iraq Leader." *Long War Journal* (Nov 7, 2008): http://www.longwarjournal.org/archives/2008/11/iraqi_troops_kill_se.php (accessed February 1, 2013).

Shanker, Thom. "Special Operations: High Profile, but in Shadow." *New York Times*, May 29, 2007. http://www.nytimes.com/2007/05/29/world/middleeast/29forces.html?_r=1& (accessed December 1, 2012).

White, Jim. "Oman 1965-1976: From Certain Defeat to Decisive Victory." Small Wars Journal. http://smallwarsjournal.com/mag/docs-temp/93-white.pdf (accessed February 1, 2013).

US Government Documents

U.S. Army Combined Arms Center. *Field Manual 3-24, Counterinsurgency.* Washington, D.C.: United States Army, 2006.

_____. *Army Docrtinal Reference Publication 5-0, The Operations Process.* Washington, D.C.: United States Army, 2012.

_____. *Army Docrtinal Reference Publication 3-0, Unified Land Operations.* Washington, D.C.: United States Army, 2012.

US Department Of Defense. *Sustaining U.S. Global Leadership: Priorities for the 21st Century Defense.* Washington, DC: January 2012.